the arrival of rain

poems
adedayo agarau

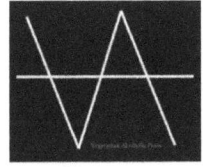

the arrival of rain ©2020 by **adedayo agarau**. published in the united states by vegetarian alcoholic press. not one part of this work may be reproduced without expressed written consent from the author. for more information, please contact vegalpress@gmail.com

cover art: *swamp thing* ©2019 by **stephanie gibart**

the arrival of rain

contents:

look how far i've come..9

entry: sometimes i am a room of stars; other times i am a corpse..10

how to love a bird right back into the sky..11

ode to cozier putting his emptiness into melody..12

baptism..13

;..14

first portrait of me as adedayo..15

second portrait as adedayo..16

a portrait of me standing by the sea..17

self portrait as a castaway..18

self-portrait as an urchin in aglow praying during maghrib..19

the wooden cross is enough prayer..20

i will one day grow to love you with my presence..21

untitled..22

the raging sea, or, tope alibis voice rides with the winds..23

an aberration..24

what it means to be freed by your country..25

a cathedral of birds..26

there are no graves for the dead..27

third portrait as adedayo..28

two weeks before my birthday..29

reflection…30

fourth portrait as adedayo, or, the barren tree at the mokola cemetery..31

fifth portrait as adedayo or as just any other child from this country..32

the origin of loss..33

milky way dirge..34

a monochrome picture of a group of people leaving home through sand rivers..35

a small dialogue about running..36

being bodies..37

calvary sri lanka..38

boy, down...39

first aubade by a mannequin dancing in the rain..40

mannequin unburnt..41

in the praises of boys that will someday not be their fathers..42

monochrome photo with my grandma's body..43

look how far i've come

                                        broken every time the door
opens
            or is banged against your face
you can count your losses but do you remember
                                        my name?

i am with you inside the room the
ground is littered with pictures   of girls who do not love
                                          you back

what better way to die   than to drown in your tears
           & while you watch their shadows evaporate
into space   through your broken window
                  i whisper   *mo ni fe're*
but you do not hear   *ololufe mi*
                  your wound is open
like my door   *fe'mi*   *fe'mi*   *fe'mi*

i am still here, mending bridges that won't stand

entry: sometimes i am a room of stars; other times i am a corpse

you remind me of the blank sky   standing vulnerable above jesus
at gethsemane, remind me of how it is easy to crumble at the feet of
a dead saviour, one betrayed by a kiss, you taste like sea in my mouth,
taste like swine, i will someday be bold enough to call myself pig, soil
your lips which harbor a colony of demons collecting stars from the hopeless body
of a distressed moon   i am in conversation with the moon-man   his
wife left him for a god that is silent in all ways and echoes of your name
     never made it home   my sister carries me inside her thoughts,
carries
my mother dreaming of coming home to pat my back in the room rancid with your name
my tired eyes are sorry for staring into the dark spot in your eyes, calling blindness a
 cloud   gathering for rain

how to love a bird right back into the sky

the chemical arsenal of a bird, a dead bird, is in its wings
a name that means a war three oceans away, a bird stands
before a mirror to reimagine itself as a gun in the head, imagine
that my fingers are not flowers today, they are not morning dews
sitting at the tip of a tongue: i remember my grandmother's first kiss,
the way it undid my mistakes, spelled my name right from the belly of a battle
this is what they mean when they say *i love you*, these girls that have measured
the width of my shaft by wrapping their lips around the tip; these girls that
have turned night into a gallery of shadows, poured a school of fishes into a glass
cup; these girls, they mean that i am nothing but a sky incapable of hugging a bird
holding tight to what i own, what i name, what i do not name, call me a bird, tell me
i have fallen in the manner that angels fell back into the wrath of the earth, tell me
that my demons grow a forest inside me, that i am a plantation of seasoned blues
tell me that i am always running; but my grandmother says that i am home, her smiles
remind me of everything that i do not own, every city i have to conquer, every breath
i have to catch, reminds me that before this mirror that spreads across the wall like a sky
i can fly

ode to hozier putting his emptiness into melody

i've heard this song before inside my dream / a bullet head / inside the boy indecent enough to undress his grief before the sea buttoned eyes / sunlight broken femurs of light bokehs / this is it:

                                      a vamp is fastened into a soaked body
                                      i've tasted this grief but never in my
                                      own tongue / today i am the boy that
                                      give names to his grief

i love this country / body / boy so much i think birds became forest trees all at once & angels are becoming demons on marble streets / i have seen that loving a girl is the cheapest way to becoming a god / a poet / a seer but moonwalking back into loving yourself / falling back into the void narrowed into your body where my body slides back / into the city won by war / i am in constant battle a shower turns into a cry show / my mother calls from outside / this is not how it should end

another unfathering
i am scrubbing my mouth
clean of your name
unbuckling every kiss with
an aubade / everything   has a way of telling me it is my father's absence
the moon is giant   in my mouth

i have made love to shadows & my body carries names of the dead / sunflowering a grave into petal

ija do pin ogun si tan halleluyah / i am lonely tonight / the windows in my body are shut against the light of your name / my mother's voice is sinking in the stream
ija do pin ogun si tan
        halleluyah / dancing / halleluyah / earth of you breathing back into the sky

baptism

12 candlesticks bounded by the grip of your hands / your knees narrowed into the marrow of silt

fire x7 / Jesus x7 / your white sultana carrying the embodiment of the sea's grief

the demons

in your body / dance / to the raging
                                songs from the music box / in your throat / if your mother
wasn't / in the picture / you would be a roadmap
                                for boys ask / ing for the life of this city / you
are the way/ truth / life / saviour
                                of the shadow's creek / tributary of desire / menace

in its own body / a river is thrown back into a sea
& to say you are / lost is to say the earth is
spher / ical / is to say the Lord is the king of this place / ghetto
in Ajegunle, a boy once / shoved
you behind the dark of a kiosk / think of paper / birds & the kites he flew / in your
body / think of a cart race & the tender / miracles falling

                                              out

                                           of

                                                your

                                                      mouth

the priest says that you are cursed by the sea / 12 candlesticks bound
by the grip of your hands / the winds shear your garment with fury your mother is miles
away / watching

the priest stares

into your cleavage

for christ's sake

;

i saddle god into my body / lift my mouth up like a flint / my wings will be a safehouse
a nest held together by old shoelaces / of my unwanted dreams

           give me a new thing to cry about / & i do not mean love
or my father's disappearance   or my mother's tears gathering to form an ocean
    i mean that if demons are pestles pounding the heads of newborns
let me be chased out of   my sleep   let me be my father's body / unsettled
    outcast / tired of everywhere / unable to sit / unable to love his past

      unable to settle himself into the ferry
      my mother still wakes to the hurt of
      his hands
           give me a new thing to cry about   not my father's
           despicable smile   or my mother
    constantly asking god to guide his feet home

first portrait of me as adedayo

let's assume the body is an estrangement
        a beach house washed up in a sea the tender waves calling calling calling
let's assume the body is a little flower
          praying for the sun pleading to be left alone in the wind alone
            with the stars in a night sky alone with the grief trapped
            in the ship of its own sea
 let's assume the body is a departure
             i dream of my grandmother's coffin, the golden handle
            and undertakers dancing her into oblivion
her dead hands twitch ocean eyes in my father's parlour

erasure: the body is not a property

i present myself holy / and broken / cast deep into the depth of my wounds / take me into your mouth give me the colony of my desolation / i just want to be a coloured boy in the dark / i just want to dance beneath a campaign of moon and wind / i just want my father to cry back into my hands / let there be a city / let god be known / this body, dead with bones, shall rise & in the lifting / my grandmother shall rise to sing me back to sleep

amen.

second portrait as adedayo

my heart blows in the dark / erased / sun moon / little lights from the mouth of a child
there is a knowing, then, a loss / i once took myself to the river to drown or end this
conversation going awry in my body

in the first portrait, i am a little boy sitting comfortably on fire / the grief
in my body growing like oak trees reaching for stars / this is it

each time i see a knife / it means a placard to me / means my name is a ferry on a lake
/ means the body is a dead thing to me / means i am entering a city blessed with fury
/ means the dogs bark at me / means i run when they don't / run when they do / still
i run / even from this prison called a body / where paper birds take flight & kites are
coloured hopes lost in clouds / i run

in this portrait / i am scared of going home / scared of taking my feet out of the water
/ the sea is a forgiving space for boys who recognize turbulence / my father calls me &
his voice bites my back / my wings are trapped / there is no going back

home

a portrait of me standing by the sea

there is no such thing as happiness
no such thing as joy like a river
the saddest people go to the sea
          there is a spirit raising placards in my body
there are demons waltzing to kiwanuka's cold little heart
this is not against my knowing

but i have lifted my head in prayer
maybe this time   *i'll be strong*
i know all bones break

into trapeziums of loneliness
          or what remains in my body when the real boy is dead

self portrait as a castaway

i have nothing else to say to myself
but this was the body cast away from
shiloh   the unanswered prayer
the baby unrepentantly dying in hannah's
womb   the priest's remorse   this
was the body casted into the swine   i
wear the cloth of a pig   i wear the
mouth of rags   this body is sour
the fallen angel with an unhealing scar

self-portrait as an urchin in agbowo praying during maghrib

                intro: from the badland of a boy's body a sweet voice wraps
                a prayer   into a plea   into a question   woven
                out the tip of his tongue & the conglomeration of his palms

       this is me / here & alive?
       brown feathers at the center of my tongue   hope is a weightless thing   like
       feathers   like sin (when i say sins i remember my father's
       grave   the dust & wildflowers are unforgiving)

my mouth is sour against this prayer   *wudu* is just a brief way of admitting
that i am dirty   my tongue is coarse against the distance my
father washed   himself before he pleaded to be
                        taken
                                  before *baba's* answered prayer became my
                                  lamentation   open wounds nursed by air

my body still translates hunger
as loss

                                still demons raging like thunderstorms clapping
                                in the same language as an angry sea   still
                                i enter the morning with a body rising into faith
                                rush out of day with starlights shimmering their
                                tender wishes   at the base of this sorrow
                                i am soft & boyish   lost

                     & not found
                     today

the wooden cross is enough prayer
for elisabeth horan

today, the woman in this poem sighs like a river
in the tired of her breathing, the wall gecko sticks
its tongue to catch a fly   is this how we die
is this how the ground becomes soft with flowers
the air hushed by silence & little kids in black
at the funeral running after each other's shadows
while they learn the concept of loss   the rain
begin to pour me back into a prayer   for you
for your body   *cut it open   spread yourself
out in the sun   maybe this place will become damascus
or the river stirred by headless angels   be paul
be the leper   be the beautiful gate & the miracle   be
the reason jesus wept*
                    the tremor shakes the church
open arms hugging vigorous prayers   the woman
in this poem is the church full of light & a graffiti of mary
crying against the wall   a choir of pain raises its voices
the way the sun does   & at the east of her body where
god placed the cervical muscles   job lived there
tried   desolated   ruined   but alive   & kicking

i will one day grow to love you with my presence

but now, i am still broken. the half empty cup. a moon eaten half by clouds. dark clouds. the sky is bitter with leaves. i am still the screamer & the voice. the echo that never made it home. i am still the shadow of a whole body or perhaps, the song dying along the pews of the cathedral. i am still the one with a pungent mouth. do not remind me that i am from a lineage of men who do not wait. who are always on the road. running from love or the appearance of happiness. do not remind me that i am my father's boy. the pendant in the pocket of his dreams.

i will one day grow to love the thorns. dead birds will float. that day is not today. i am still on the road. my feet are burning with disappearance. o' lover. o' girl that shines like a polished sea, the sun hears your tears. but i, my father blocked my ear!

untitled.

this way, i commit myself to the cross / i love the way i die / as a son / no longer slave to stars / a galaxy of singers gathering momentum in me / i can be all music & deaf / the earth is a spaceship of grief farmers / my father's absence was our first harvest / my mother held a brown leaf to her mouth the same way a bird gathers a nest / this poem is not for my mother / salt in the bathtub / my mother's sobs slipping from under the bathroom door / into the room / my friends called our house a studio of broken echoes / the songs that never made it home hang on the wall as pictures / they are sometime unwhole memories / dagger in the chest of a new born / my sister, tender & toddling / learned to say *baba* before she could spell the names of shadows who have bodies / my mother's face is a sea of drowned ancestors / i can tell that her unhappinesses are helium balloons in the sky / a god crucified by a kiss hangs around her head / grief is what we have in common / but i am never home to name my losses:

> my first lover called me a moss / that is to mean that i do not have life & i am a language found between blisters & bombs / an ungathered home without a father figure / all my sorrows find a way to remind me that there are stars falling out of my sky / that i will have to carry an ark & invite god into it

> my name is *adedayo* / that is crown becomes joy / but i carry a coronet nursed by slaves / means i am a diadem in the mud / means i am music in the mouth of a boy lost in a city / the priest laid his hands on me & called me royal / my body feels like it is a city under a siege / a gun to my head is not a gun / it is my family dragging me back into oblivion / my father's name, *agarau* / means pride means greatness means to be a boy & be a king means to be proud in the way i cry / means horses ride my body / means light is dead & i have to walk the earth in the dark / means i wear a galaxy of depression & my first lover is right / i am the moss from a forgotten linage / my father is gone / drowned in wadi while crossing the sea / & his name drowned with it

the raging sea, or, tope alabi's voice rides with the winds

1. *you shall receive power when the holy ghost comes upon you* / my body is an empty house / a chimney of nothingness / i am cold flames in blue fire / & you shall rise like dust / & your laughter shall call water out from rocks / & your house shall no longer be empty / my mother sings to me in my dream / brings a candlestick stick to light the dark tunnels in my vein / i saw the lord riding a chariot of tongues / my mother was with the host of good news / all of them decked in white / *erujeje erujeje erujeje*

2. i am son of shackles / a bloodline of shadow & myth / a tongue is nothing but a compass on the map of the mouth & there i was too / a lost boy crumbled by his own fear / for light for absence for love / & the kiss does not mean an actual death / my mother kissed my father & stayed / kissed him & turned her body into a miracle of children / i am son of bondage / hear the glass cracking in my body / hear the rising of the sea / *adaba mimo emi orun* / i am son of sky / blue with sin / red with names owned by the ground / the serpent came to teach me how to speak / the son turned

3. my tongue into knife / cut himself for christ's sake / bled out the boy crumbling in me

4. a woman with an issue of blood was made whole / while jesus walked through the old walkway / i touched him

5. i wear a crown in this poem / not a coronet for slaves or a thorn / not a brass holding my wings back to the ground / i wear a son / not a child

an aberration

the night my dog died
i was still four   & the widow
from the other house screeched
              in her sleep again

my mother folded her arms
against her chest   as if
she held the outbreak of silence
                 so keenly

loss is like a wind that touches
everything   the sand in my mouth
did not grow any flowers
                   that year

what it means to be freed by your country
for Daniel Usman

daniel, 19, opens his head for a dozen bullets. the bulletin
says his body is a prize, a man shows the president his prey,
a man takes the street into his mouth, turns a rose into a coin,
a boy's head becomes a headline, democracy ties a knot with
silence, the sun sinks beneath the tongue, the moon wedges
itself behind the clouds, the boy will someday rise into a
revolution, men revolting against a country that asks for heads
instead of thumbs, blood instead of nods, this is my country,
a jungle of men breaking out of the night. somewhere in lagos,
a man says the only way to power is showing what you have killed,
says in this country, the body is nothing but a count, a score, another
boy falls back into his father's hands, dead, in ibadan, his mother
boils with fury, a field of revenge rises in her eyes. this is how we cast
our innocence in a ballot of anguish, how birds burn the chimney in the sky.
my country is ocean's exit wounds, and to be free means to be
caged in a coffin, to ride home as a boy, 19, with trumpets and despair,
thinking, this, my country, a city under siege, served my father a plate of my dead body.

a cathedral of birds

i come from a long line of women who teach their sons
how to disassemble their laughter

turn a circus into a spike, a song into a mob,
a church into a funeral

i rise from the city where flowers grow out of salt
sprinkled on an open wound

where the sun cooks the dead again as if the ground wasn't a dress
enough, as if prayers gone into the winds are mere kites lost in confetti

i come from memory, the shore
where desires are little sand castles

the field where i had my first kiss
where a moth grew into a butterfly

was where the ground first tasted blood
where a bullet smothered your head into

a nest. I come from a place where we do not forget
where we walk like shadows in our own bodies

where the dead are not dead until their graves carry
more than one boy, where a funeral can sometimes

become a reunion, a church, a school, a garden
of flowers, where we remember that a boy is just

a boy, nothing else, not a church, a cathedral,
where we liken his head to a nest full of bullets.

there are no graves for the dead
    for Ladipo, Solanke, Okezie

an indolent cloud broke out of the sky that morning
a flower rode out of a cracked wall the dead will
speak of turning, will speak of growing back into
history, into the feet of a boy half worn by dreams
of dust & of a country crumbled into a sea

the morning the war began, my father sat in his chair
rocking the radio impatiently against his ear

somewhere else, a body tinged by rain was set ablaze
this means that someone burned for his country   that
person was my uncle, that person was a native man twisted by language

& so what if we were briefly beautiful, if this country was a sea
& now it's still a sea & now, people are rushing against the waves
& now, we are eaten by soldiers hungry for bodies, hungry for power

my mother screamed from the kitchen, her sister & her family
were shot in the head for the colour of their language in kano
she trembled down the hallway like a leaf in the wind

my father said we are far from trouble, the jungle
where bullets drizzle down the body of a town   where nothing
is calm & everything is a people rushing back into incineration

we sat around the table & held hands
my mother was reciting the rosary when they came for my father
they dragged his body like taboo before blowing his head against the sitting room wall

a machete found shelter between the chest of a woman crying for freedom
for a country where children grow into a bedrest for haunting memories

third portrait as adedayo

my shadow carries another sunrise on its back
still, there is no ounce of light in the corner

of my mouth. my skin is bruised by silt & truth,
the edge of sky, of moons bleeding into clouds

like lamps dashing into flames before dawn.
i am made of journeys, footprints of ghosts

showing a boy the path to the sea, where
they drowned, where lovers clung to lovers

& language became men gulping an island of water
i am not my father but we have the same face

my mother sounds like me & i sound like the sea;
the raging waters beating against the rock

i am battered & boyish

(read from bottom to top & top to bottom)

two weeks before my birthday

i.
as we fucked
lights out
                the bed shook like
                a tree tormented

                                  by rain
            your name
      hid the shame in my mouth

the doorway was open
                              i cried black into your back
kissed your neck
                drove you crazy   drove you out of my mind

& as the day bled into nightfall
                          everything crumbled into the ground
you said, *i'm cumming ade*

                    i am still waiting for the arrival of rain

ii.
for light's sake / i pluck moon from the sky and place it in this poem / no girl loves a poet as his drafts do / i remember reading you my poem about cunnilingus before flapping your clit with the leaflet of my tongue / i remember how the room wore your mouth / how you turned like the hand of a clock & guided me into the bowels of your body with your hand / but that is not enough to mourn you / not suitable / to decipher how beauty can mean *iku* in another language

iii.
i want to be left alone
                            i carry a bible to go in search of god
all i see is a museum   a little light   & another little light
                  falling out of the holes you used to fill with your throat

reflection

i.
goodness & / mercy / shall follow you / all the days of your life
& you shall be a boy / not a sting /
not a spear in the sun / & you shall be a song
that made it out of an abandoned throat
not a tantrum / not an ancient walkway / not a crack

ii.
the cross is also a boy bleeding inside / a room / is also a ghost giving earth a
new / name / this is not about those who left the door open / is about those whose
shadows hold the door hostage / i do not mention my own father / do not mention me
as the boy in this poem / do not wake the sleeping body of my mother / the earth is
already full of wailers / the door stands between loss & settlement / my father who is a
bullet fired at the sun / came back to hunt the fingers / i want to forget how to carry
something you do not own

iii.
didn't jesus die for people who can't stand alone? those whose shadows lean against
the wind. those who live in houses where there are more pictures than there are walls.
the flowers blooming by the window are a story of how a man who wakes to water
them is gone with the winds. the silence, the silence here is the afterparty of genocide. &
no one is dead yet. we are just lost within ourselves. didn't jesus die for the boy whose
prayers are swallowed by geckos too?

fourth portrait as adedayo, or, the barren tree at the mokola cemetery

what is this the lord has given to me?
        cherry wine in hozier's mouth or
                the blade dreaming of john's head
either way
            i die
either way
        the boy is reimagining death as the blooming of flower
        as the day he harvests the deflated memories of unreachable things

either way
        the postcards buried in the cupboard behind the kitchen will be read
        to other boys   girls will giggle or fall away like wilted leaves
        when they hear their names

this gospel will breathe back into me
                            clouds raising placards against the coming of rain
god can you see what you made?
                            boys once bitten by the serpent in eden will
never tender an apology for being lost
                            can you hear my mother rocking her face against
the wall, the affliction in her throat
how every song dies before
first lines form like first men like
                        first sins?
                        everything is death when the sun is sleeping
a boy hanging from a tree reads
a testament aloud
        god, do you
                        know what it means to hide pain beneath the skin?
what does it mean to say a word
and be misunderstood?
                        i re-imagine myself as a choir singing a cathedral
out of my father's little wounds
                        i re-imagine every house as a fire singeing a boy's
        skin
              water the tree when you find the boy in this poem

fifth portrait as adedayo or as just any other child from this country

when someone dies, a child, of course, my heart feels bigger than this country
like it is my duty to carry all our grief on my shoulder because i am my father's
child, because this is only sand i have tasted, because this is the place i landed
when my mother's bowels opened into a bowl of broken water, a head swimming
out of the flower room. i pushed a banderner into my friend's bullet wound because
that's the wisest thing to do because i would rather nurse a wound than nurse a dead
 boy
in my heart than clean for a gallery of dying butterflies than watch his mother fly
over the bridge than hang a ghost on my wall & remember how we turned sand into
homes for our feet than say *you promised to be my sunrise*

the origin of loss

there is nothing as lucid as a dead boy / & his mother kneeling beside the halved moon leaking out of his body / a shadow sinking into the ground / a fainting of bird songs / the crow's absence from the morning is an adage / the sun sits with the clouds / gulps a bowl of blood / draws a circumference with his mother's tears / isn't that / everything? / in a country where we all wear the same skin / a man who mourns the night with his body pulls the trigger / a boy whose dreams are pleasant flowers & sunbeams / minarets & clarinets / falls / isn't / that everything / to mourn or be mourned in this market where we all are music in someone's throat / ? / on my grandfather's farm a bird fell off a tree / i remember it today / the silence to come after the thud / synagogue stacked with dead choirs / the mother of the boy sits beside her son and cries / there is nothing said that will take that loss away

milky way dirge

memory is a flowery place
if we do not have to deal with
the past. & a ray of light

from a truck spilled on
the windscreen of my father's car
like milk upon a shirt, light became water

all over the screen, no one saw
what came. & the memory takes me
back to the evening —where i begin again

where i count the number of countries
that have a name & a sea in them & try to remember their capitals
—a father throws his son in the air
as if pledging him to the angels
as if asking him to take flight
his hands readily waiting to receive
whatever the air gives back to him as a son

—but i remember, nonetheless, how
we merged our faith together, my mother and i,
in that room of people pacing with silent prayers
asking the nurses to remember, saying their
lovers' names all over while death grabbed his neck & pulled his breath out

a monochrome picture of a group of people leaving home through sand rivers

we, a people running to sand river
with exit wounds and bloodlines
morphing the sins promised by our fathers
into distance, into images of butterflies
cracking in fire, into a space between language
and trembling fingers,

petals blooming, matching colours with names
because there is a certain fire in our homes
pushing us to the road, asking our feet to rush

& in the eye of the sun, a boy incinerates
& there is no bed to please his body with
we write his epitaph with a candlestick and a bowl of sand

a people casting their sins at the door of masjid
in zawiyah snatched our names and called us slaves
because all things that have a soul must be named
because all things that have a soul must be named
me, my father, and the body of that boy buried in the sand

a small dialogue about running

in kubwa, this is how women match
the night with their grief:
they go back into the village whose walls
opened for staccato of bullets
one goes into her house to find her husband's head split into a blend

the others are on the field, asking why their boys
became cheap motels for death

when war comes, a mother will call her child's name
before she takes to her heels

the river will split for stories of people asking us never to return
a daughter will fall off her mother's back
the pandemonium in her cries will be stilled by a stampede

some men will stand and say,
"this is my fathers' land,
we will not forsake home
we will not forsake home"

their bodies will give up ghosts
when cutlasses find rest in their necks

being bodies

time is a lousy shadow // the image on the wall
is your figure slim shady the audible passage of moments
loud in my ears & slowly you chime into distance fading //
the threnody of water soaked in the eyes of our dreams
the ones we incubated as we emptied ourselves into ourselves //
in secret // say love is what my father carried in his chest //
say my mother is fat with all the times they have made love //
say she carried the evidence casting fingers into his mouth //
but we are two cities splitting into towns // the earth becomes
livid with memories and in our bones we twitch to music
we twitch to love we twitch to the making of butterflies
sometimes i ask the wall how it is easy for it to stay how
i wake each morning to find it waiting but we are bodies
// quickened by departures & the blood in our veins boils for others
& mouth dreams of a new mouth // say i got tired of dreaming of night
ghouls // say you got tired of me walking in and out
barging silence against the door flirting with fingers and numbness
in my room i still listen to your voicenotes your voice asks me to come home
but i'm faraway in a town full of birds perching on my lips

calvary sri lanka

half moon, a night held down by owls
& trap songs beating the dark back to life &
crickets crunching shadows the way
the pharynx folds a song neatly inside the throat
& this song will never make it to his mouth, this boy
that marked the first blood, this boy whose body is the beginning
of siege: how a city opens itself for bullets, a throat to a knife, a
little flower wilts in silence, unlike jesus, this boy does not
protest, does not die asking to breath, or for a miracle,
this boy lays beside the church, emptying blood
for ground to gulp, and after this boy,
the church's door opens & the men who
have come to harvest breaths walk into the
house of god with barrels strapped at their backs,
they open fire as if it was an answered prayer, as if to wait
upon the lord is to dine with him, his body swollen with revenge
for every time each man in sri lanka has denied him, as if everyone
at the church bear peter, the moon halved by dirge now hides
its sunburned cheek beneath the specks of dust, christ has risen
with the bodies of sinners & saints, a city is raptured and
in a church the pastor asked to break bread
to drink of the blood that flows out of these bodies, to
open the ground & bury themselves for all have sinned.

boy, down

                                                      this grief,
                                                     is perhaps,
                                                         in music

                                                   how i forsake
                                                 my own body
                                            once the dirge

                                                       starts //

              i once turned my love towards a girl that turned
                   water to water & called it a miracle
                       her tongue rocked against my ear
                         merged silence into silence
                           called herself a goddess

in an evening while the sky ate the winds
i entered my father's *kembe*
because my body felt like a stampede
of virgins flying winglessly above the sea

blue sea // salt earth // i carry my wounds home to my father // *see, this is a testament
of my war // call me a soldier, father //* butterflies flushing down my father's eyes // a
concerto crashing into silence

                                            to love a boy that loves the grave
                             is to nurse the wounds of sky
the way rain nurses the earth with its tears
                                   //
loss begins by feeling out of home &
in a room where the rosary falls
beside the candle
                   i know god has fallen against its light in this part of my body
& all i want is its ghost knocking the wall of this room where a monochrome photo
of all my goodbyes hang on the wall
                                    all i want is to take my body from this fire
to reclaim all the territories eaten by grief
saddle my lips back to laughter

                         this grief,
                         is perhaps,
                         in music

                  my grandmother's shadow
                  sings itself back to grave.

first aubade by a mannequin dancing in the rain

i feel nothing but beautiful
                 my body is the crossroad where god turned water to languages
gracious god
                 the east of this body pushes old bones deep into god's nose
i can sing too
                 i imagine how many tears the rock would've shed if Noah had
                 cut it an onion
still,
                 in the shade where girls are lemon stars & the emptiness of open
        palms
                 i carry a name from a stranger's grave
still,
                 a bruised body is a basket / i bleed each time i carry anything
                 i feel too heavy to be tagged a house
today, i am my father's son
                 but never his child / it is the same way you unwrap a seed
                 & never find the germ

                 i plant myself in the rain / gracious god / waiting for the sky to
swallow me in small doses / in the tiny bits that language comes to the
                 knowing of tongues / the same way the night draws you back
to the same light you are rushing from / i do not trust any promise of
                 light / every light that leads the way can blind the eyes / i
squint as i pledge my allegiance to this god crucifying my body

mannequin unburnt

the foreword to this poem is a boy bleeding his anguish back into the sky:
revelations have it that we are fallen stars   i imagine my brother & i holding
hands   naming each stone after our bruises   after our wounds   after
every hand that ever laid back its wrath into the ribcages of our soul   reve-
lation also has it that we are sea, a blue sky with paper boats, little children surfing
kites against the rebellions of wind, over the mothers of sea   my mother begged
us never to look into walls   never to cast a stone against the sea   said her
father
still breathing   would someday bring the riches of salt back to us in this room
still my brother & i hold hands   it should count as prayer   it should count
as a rebellion against gods drowned in water   teaching mothers to wear their
children a marasmic faith   in church where water was first named purity
a girl suckled on my tongue   & nothing happened & i sucked her back where she
ached the most in this poem   i unmake every distance my tongue has ever
covered   erase the paths it has cleansed   she spit her name into
my ear
& mixed it with fallacy
                      we burn   as silent gods housed in our bodies
as knowledge as wisdom of days covered without water as the blessings of dew
my
rosary breaks during prayer god should be stronger next time   my brother holds me
still   & he is the only god that i bend to

in the praises of boys that will someday not be their fathers

my father once showed us about rapture & how a ghost
will one day rise like smoke leaving the sea for the sky & that everything
gone will someday return as rain
         my mother cried us a lamb
cried us a house without windows in which the children are little flies
in which i am the lamp dying by the edge of the room in which
there was a father who raised his voice instead of raising his boys in
which everything gifted with time will end crushing the flowers growing
boys like me are next to the sea we are seashells drowned by footprints
in sand   in our mother's name   in a house in which its light no
longer
glows

monochrome photo with my grandma's body

a boy's body is a border / between memory, where everything is undone / & pictures
& in this picture, i stand beside a grave / a father's mother whose mouth is a loose bird
whose body is a wall crushed by misfired bullets / whose hands are never at home
i mean, i stand beside the entourage of war / a cacophony of owls crashing into the
composition / the aperture leading us to the inside of a house where a father is absent
but still smelled like gun fired against a chest / a woman is down, longing behind the
photographer / i stand beside silence, a woman numbed from remembering how a
hand once tender like soil grew into a glass of stale wine / my throat disgorges every
slice of his name / my grandmother reminds me that i have his smile / reminds me that a
father gone or trapped in the winds / is a feather / is a dirge

Adedayo Adeyemi Agarau is a Nigerian poet and documentary photographer. He is a graduate of Human Nutrition. Adedayo was shortlisted for the Babishai Niwe Poetry Prize in 2018, Runner up of the Sehvage Poetry Prize, 2019. He was the runner-up of the Eriata Oribhabor Poetry Prize, 2017. Adedayo is the Assistant Editor for Poetry at *Animal Heart Press*, the Contributing Editor for Poetry at *Barren Magazine*. His works have appeared or are forthcoming on *Gaze, Glass, Jalada Africa, 8 Poems, Hellebore, Headway Lit, Nitrogen House* and elsewhere. Adedayo is curating and editing a Nigerian Poetry Anthology. His chapbook, *Origin of Names*, was selected by Chris Abani and Kwame Dawes for African Poetry Book Fund, 2020.

www.ingramcontent.com/pod-product-compliance
Lightning Source LLC
Chambersburg PA
CBHW020029040426
42333CB00039B/864